Matt Mullins' Basic Tricks

The 1st step-by-step book & DVD
on acrobatics for martial artists

By
Matthew Mullins

For martial arts instructors,
competitors and enthusiasts.

Matt Mullins' Basic Tricks
The 1st step-by-step book on acrobatics for
martial artists, volume 1
(Book and DVD)

By **Matthew Mullins**

Published by
High Mountain Publishing
California, USA
www.howtotrick.com

Printed in Korea

International Standard Book Number
Paperback Edition
0-9718609-7-1

First Printing
July 2006

Book Layout, Design
& Photography
Ursula Escher

Models for Photography
Chris Brewster
Craig Henningsen
Jackson Spidell
Leo Howard
Matthew Mullins
Michelle Mix

DISCLAMER
The techniques shown in this book may
cause injury. Be sure to consult your
physician before engaging in this or any
exercise program.

This book is dedicated to all the amazing instructors and students with whom I've had an opportunity to work. I am truly honored to take what I have learned and pass it on to the next generation of champions.

Special Thanks to Sensei Sharkey, Mike Chat, Dr. Dave Smith, Craig Henningsen, Chris Brewster, Jackson Spidell, and all the fans of Sideswipe!

CONTENTS

by **Matthew Mullins**

Intro

MARTIAL ARTS, COMPETITION, TRICKING AND YOU
BEING YOUR BEST
USING THIS BOOK

01 Martial Arts Competition, Tricking and You

Why is competition beneficial to martial arts training?

Competition has been around for hundreds of years. Historically, competition was used as a way to settle disputes between countries. As times have changed, so has competition. Martial art tournaments nowadays host a huge array of different divisions; everything from forms and fighting, to knife throwing and weapon forms. Most recently, extreme (acrobatic) forms divisions have been introduced.

There are a lot of people who say competition and tricking "is not real" or "something you would never do in the streets". Honestly, they are right! Competition and tricking are not a street fight, they are a sport! They are recreation! They are ways to exhibit skill, learn from other styles and art forms, and to express yourself creatively. I personally have found competition to be very rewarding, and the greatest tool to push my skills above and beyond levels I never thought I could reach.

Sideswipe performing at the AKA Grand Nationals, 2004.

What is Tricking?

Tricking is flashy techniques. Anything beyond a practical self defense technique is a trick. Martial artists looking to push themselves physically and creativity have dreamed up many tricks. Tricks have a flair from all different styles of martial arts, acrobatics, and various performance styles. Tricks have been added to enhance overall difficulty and dynamics to every extreme competition routine and performance. Even though a lot of tricks have an acrobatic flavor to them, they should all have a martial art base with a kick, block, or punch. If not, you are no longer performing martial arts, but a gymnastic routine.

Is Tricking right for me?

Tricking is not only doing a movement, but also an attitude and energy that you give to all of your techniques. I believe that anyone can learn to trick, as long as they continue to work at it correctly, safely and diligently.

Matt with Mike Chat after winning the AKA Warrior Cup in 1999.

Team USA at the 1997 WKA world Championships.

02 Being your best

Matt winning 5th WKA (World Karate Association) gold medal.

Applying Yourself

This book is just a guide to help you learn new techniques and reach your goals. If you are looking for the ultimate answer on 'how to win', you will never find a book or an instructor with all the right answers. The real trick to being your best is to have an open mind, learn as much as you can, focus on all of the things that help you, and forget the rest.

Everyone learns in a different way. You have to find how you learn best, and do that. I hope I can give you some insight into what I have learned over the past 15 years to help you be your best!

03 Using this book

Throughout this book you will find icons that highlight important sections:

 Caution. Be extra careful and take extra time during your training.

 Training Tips you don't want to miss. Improve your technique by paying attention to detail.

 Important advice to help beginners who are learning new techniques and tricks for the first time.

Matt with Team USA Ireland WKA World Championships 1996.

Matt with Instructor John Sharkey and Soaps Long after winning his second WKA World Title.

Warm-up

RAISE YOUR HEART RATE

WARM UP YOUR CORE

FIRING MAJOR MUSCLE GROUPS

Warm up Routine at a glance

1 raise your heart rate >>>

Jumping Jacks *p17*

Jogging 1 *p18*

Jogging 2 *p19*

2 warm up your core >>>

Waist Rotations *p21*

Shoulders *p22*

Neck Stretches *p23*

Knees 1 *p24*

Knees 2 *p25*

Ankle Stretch *p26*

Wrist Stretch *p27*

3 firing major muscle groups >>>

Lunges
p29

Squats 1
p30

Squats 2
p31

Squats 3
p32

Squats 4
p33

Leg Swing 1
p34

Leg Swing 2
p35

Hip Swing
p36

Hamstring Stretch
p37

Hip Flexor Stretch
p38

Shoulders Stretch
p39

01 Raise your Heart Rate

I know stretching can be boring and dull, but flexibility and conditioning are the essential foundation to elevate your tricking to the next level. Proper warm up will help you trick safely and help prevent injury.

Most traditional stretching is static (not moving), which is good when you are cooling down. When warming up for tricking, we want to improve our dynamic range of motion, so we need an active stretching program. Active stretches combine motion and flexibility, which increases blood flow to help warm up and stretch muscle groups simultaneously.

Imagine taking a thin strip of caramel, placing it in the freezer, taking it out, and then trying to bend it. What happens? It snaps! Now imagine taking another piece of caramel, placing it in the oven for five minutes, and then trying to bend it. The caramel stretches and moves the way you want it. A funny example, but very similar to the reason why you want to warm up your muscles before you stretch.

Let's start with Jumping Jacks. The same ones you learned to do in school. Why? They are one of the most effective exercises you can do to raise your heart rate and prepare your body to move through its full range of motion.

Jumping Jacks

I would recommend doing **75 to 100** to really get your body moving and warm for all the activities ahead.

▶ Start feet together and hands to the side.

Jump and spread your feet apart while bringing your hands together above your head.

Hop again to your start position. ◆

Jogging 1

20 steps in one place each foot

▶ This exercise is done to start moving your hamstrings (back of thighs) through some range of motion, and to continue to raise your heart rate.

Jog in place by bringing your knees up to your waist. ◆

Jogging 2

▶ This exercise is to start warming up your quads (top of legs).

Now with each step kick your feet back to touch your butt. ◆

02 Warm up your core

Matt and Chris Brewster on the set of 'Blood Fist 2050', 2005.

In this section we will perform active stretches targeting your core. Your core is your bodies stabilization system. Every time you step, turn, or kick you are using your core. The core consists of approximately 29 muscles, but more simply it is your abs and lower back. In this section we will also warm up connective joints such as your knees, ankles, shoulders.

Waist Rotations

5 full rotations in each direction

▶ This stretch is mostly for your hips and lower back.

Place your hands on your hips. Keep your feet planted and rotate your waist in a circle. ◆

Shoulders

▶ Start with your shoulders relaxed.

Roll your shoulders up towards your ears, to the back, and then all the way through to the front. ◆

Neck Stretches

5 reps each direction

▶ Look up and look down.   Look Left and look Right.   Ears to shoulders Left and Right.   Full circle both ways. ◆

Knees 1

▶ Start with your knees and feet towards the front and place your hands on your knees.

Open your legs as if you were going to do a butterfly strech in the air.

Straighten them out to full standing and return to the start position. ◆

Knees 2

▶ Keep your knees together this time and place your hands on your knees.

Rotate in a full circle bending your knees at the most forward point and then straightening them to full standing position. ◆

Ankle

5 reps each direction

▶ Rotate your foot through its full range of motion. ◆

Wrist Stretches

1 stretch forward each wrist and 5 rolls each direction

▶ Grab your fingers and lock your elbow keeping the arm straight. Pull your fingers towards your chest to stretch the arm and wrist. ◆

▶ Clasp hands and roll wrists in a circle through their full range of motion. ◆

03 Firing major muscle groups

The next drills are designed to fire your major muscle groups in your legs. These muscle groups will be the primary movers of your legs as we begin tricking.

Lunges

▶ Start in a forward position.

Bend your knees until your back knee is an inch off the ground. Return to start position. ◆

⚠ Place most of the weight on your back leg. Bend **90 degrees** at your knees. Make sure that your knees do not go pass your toes on your front foot. Keep your hips to the front.

Squats 1

8-10 squats

▶ Start with your feet wider then shoulder width apart.

Bend your knees as low as you can without lifting your heels off the ground and without rounding your back.

Straighten your knees and return to start position. ◆

Squats 2

8-10 squats.

▶ Same exercise but this time start with your feet shoulder width apart. Hands up to a guard position and feet pointing straight. Keep your back straight.

Bend your knees as low as you can without lifting your heels off the ground and without rounding your back.

Straighten your knees and return to start position. ◆

Squats 3

10 squats each side

▷ This warm-up is a good lateral movement exercise. Start with your feet wider then shoulder width apart. Perform a squat.

As you raise up, shuffle feet to the side and perform squat.

Repeat the exercise by going from side to side. ◆

Squats 4

10 squats each side.

▶ Start with hands to the sides. Perform a squat by bending the outside leg and straightening the leg closest to the inside.

As you raise up, shuffle feet to the other side and perform the same squat. Outside leg bent and inside leg straight.

Repeat exercise by going from side to side. ◆

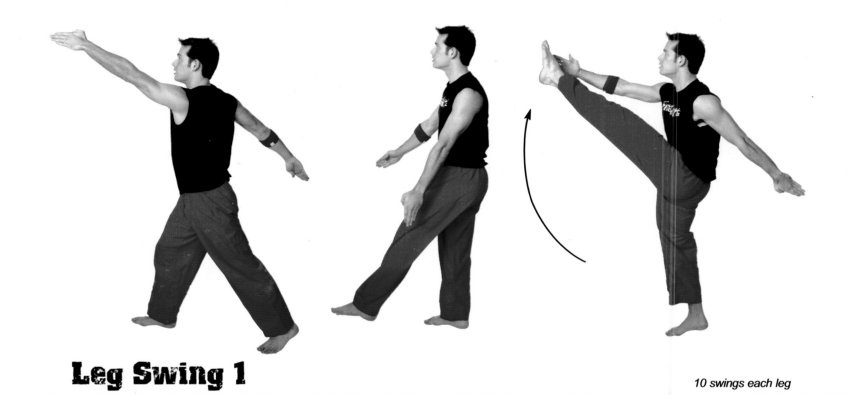

Leg Swing 1

▶ Leg swings warm you up by moving your leg through its full range of motion, and by using your stabilizing muscles to balance yourself.

Start with your feet four lengths apart. Hands in line with your back leg.

Keeping your hips forward swing your leg up while switching your hands to maintain balance.

Return to start position and repeat in a continous motion. ◆

Leg Swing 2

▶ Start with your feet together and both of your hands pointing to the direction you will swing your leg.

Bring your leg up horizontally and swing your hands to the opposite side.

Swing the leg back past the start position and repeat in a continous motion. ◆

Hip Swing

10 rolls each leg to the front
10 rolls each leg to the back

▶ Start in a forward position. Hands up.

Bring your knee up to the front and begin to roll it to the back while you push yourself off the ground with your opposite leg.

Bring your knee all the way to the back returning to the start position. ◆

Hamstring Stretch

10 reps each side.

▶ Start with your legs spread two times shoulder length apart. Hands on the ground. Drop down to one side touching your outside elbow to the ground.

Return to center and go to the other side. ◆

Hip Flexor Stretch

Hold 10 seconds each side.

▶ Start in a lunge. Keep your back leg straight.

To deepen the stretch, try to drop your hip and bring up the arm on the same side as the bent leg. ◆

Shoulders Stretch

Hold 10 seconds each side.

▶ In a horse stance, place your hands on your knees and rotate your shoulder forward.

Repeat on the other side. ◆

Kicks

01 Basics

If you have ever taken martial arts, these are the first moves you learn. Although I am sure you are ready to jump into Jackknives and Corkscrews, it is very crucial to start with a proper foundation to support and enhance all of your tricking.

I know you might have heard this a lot, but flash is trash without basics. So let's take time to review what's most important- the basics. They will help you trick faster, more effectively, and safer!

Before we start, there are many different ways to execute basic kicks. The way you throw each kick will have a different effect on its strength, speed, and control. For example, doing a Front Kick with your heel out might work great for breaking a board, but most likely won't look as good during a Trick.

I will explain what I believe is the fastest, safest and most effective way to perform basics to help you reach a higher level of kicking and tricking. If you previously learned basics a different way, don't try to unlearn anything. Just learn new ways to perform them. This will make you a more versatile martial artist.

Breathing

One aspect of tricking that is rarely touched upon is breathing. Practicing to breath out on every move is crucial. If you don't practice, you will begin to hold your breath when you throw harder moves, and you will become winded very quickly. It would be like trying to run while holding your breath. It is tough, but breathe out on every move.

Kicks at a glance

1 standing kicks >>>

Front Kick
p44

Round Kick
p46

Side Kick
p48

Hook Kick
p52

Straight Inside Crescent Kick
p56

Straight Outside Crescent Kick
p58

Snap Inside Crescent Kick
p60

Snap Outside Crescent Kick
p62

Axe Kick
p64

Skip Front Kick
p68

Front Kick

When you start to work on your Front Kick, kick low and work your way up slowly. Here are other important notes:

 Be careful not to rise up on the toes of your base foot. You may get the kick a few inches higher, but you will be unbalanced and less powerful.

Try to keep your hips straight. While trying to kick higher, you might pivot on the base foot. This is one of the only kicks you don't turn your hips over on, because the Front Kick is used primarily as a transitional move into jump kick combinations. Keeping your hips straight on the ground will also translate into keeping your hips straight on your Skip Front Kick and Jump Front Kick.

Don't swing the leg up or down. On the high Front Kick it might be easier to swing, especially down. Remember to do all 3 steps (knee up, kick, pull back) no matter what height.

 Watch out for **floppy foot syndrome** when trying to *stick* your kicks. Floppy foot is exactly how it sounds, as you lock your kick, the leg stops moving but the foot shakes.

Front Kick

If you have taken martial arts, this is probably the first kick you learned. Let's re-cap!

1 Start in Forward Stance, hips forward. Keep your hands up for balance.

2 Raise knee up.

3 Snap and **pull back.** Set down.

⚠ **Be careful not to hyper extend!**

Round Kick

The Round Kick is a very important basic kick. It is the catalyst to half of all the spinning moves you will do. Once again, there are 3 steps (knee up, kick, pull back). In order to turn your hips over for greater extension and power, be sure to point your toes and pivot on the base foot.

Round Kick

▶ Start in Side Fighting Stance.

Raise your knee to the front. Be sure your knee is pointing the way you want your kick to go. It should be pointing to the front.

Extend the leg. Point your toes. Pivot your base foot when kicking for extention and power.

Retract and set down. ◆

⚠ Be sure to keep your core muscles (abs and lower back) tight. You will lose balance and control if your butt sticks out or if you lean too far back.

Side Kick

The Side Kick is one of my personal favorite kicks. It has great power and strength. This kick has more variations than any other basic kick. The most common variable is the chambering of the leg. Some styles prepare from the knee (Japanese styles), some prepare with their leg pulled back to their chest, and others throw it like a Round Kick, but with the knife edge of the foot.

This kick is done with the knife edge of your foot (which is the outside edge of your foot). Be sure your toes are pulled back. If you have trouble getting your foot into that position, try to position it on the ground first then kick.

Personally I like to throw my Side Kick by prepping at the knee (Japanese), but the most common is a cross of both the Japanese and Korean Side Kicks.

The hand movements we use in this basic kick are to make a strong transition from a stance to the kick. Be sure you do your hand movement as strong as you kick.

Side Kick

▶ Start in a Side Fighting Stance with your hand prepared to chop.

Extend the arm and chop with a Knife Hand Strike.

Slide your back foot to your front. Pull your hand back and vertical Knife Hand Strike.

Bring the knee up like you are going to throw a Front Kick in the direction your hips are facing.

Extend the leg. Pivot your base foot while kicking for extension and power. Retract. Set it down. ◆

Hook Kick

I like to think of the Hook Kick as the Yang of all Round Kicks (which are the Yin). That's because it is almost the exact opposite of a Round Kick.

ⓘ **Different locking:** With the hook kick you will not practice the locking on the extention of the kick, but you will hold it up after you retract to show proper positioning.

Hook Kick

▶ Start in a Side Fighting Stance. Raise the leg, aiming the knee at the 45⁰ angle.

Extend the leg to the 45⁰ angle, use your hips to pull across to the other 45⁰ angle and retract.

Be sure to keep your core muscles (abs and lower back) tight. You will lose balance and control if your butt sticks out or you lean too far back.

When you do this kick correctly the knee of the kicking leg and heel of the base leg will be pointing towards the 90⁰ angle. Set down. ◆

Crescent Kicks

Crescent Kicks are the easiest kick to start tricking with because you don't need to rotate your hips at all (This will make more sense when we get to Tornado Kicks and Jump 360 Crescent Kicks). They are a great starting drill to get the mechanics of tricks. The drawback of Crescent Kicks is that they don't show your lines as well as the Hook or Round Kick.

No locking with Crescent Kicks.

We are going to work on both the Inside and Outside Crescent Kick with two variations. One is with the leg straight and the second is with the leg bent. You will use both as you start tricking. Straight leg shows off better lines. Bent will help you kick faster.

 When we talk about lines it is in reference to your body positioning. There are a lot of ways to show good lines. Generally, if you can draw a straight line through your technique, and your body positioning is straight, you will have good lines.

Leo practicing Outside Crescent Kick.

Straight Inside Crescent Kick

▶ Start in Forward
Stance, hips forward.

Swing your leg up to the
outside of your body at a
45° angle.

Use your hips to pull the leg across the front.

You will end with the kick across the body.

Place the leg back in the Forward Stance. ◆

Straight Outside Crescent Kick

▶ Start in Forward
Stance, hips forward.

Swing your leg up to the inside
of your body at a 45° angle.

Use your hips to pull the leg across the front.

As you reach the opposite 45° angle, continue to swing the leg back.

Set down. ◆

Snap Inside Crescent Kick

▷ Start in Forward
Stance, hips forward.

The knee will come up to
the outside of your body
at a 45^0 angle.

Extend the leg.

Use your hips to pull the leg across the front.

As you reach just inside the opposite 45^0 angle, retract the leg.

Set down. ◆

Snap Outside Crescent Kick

▶ Start in Forward Stance, hips forward.

The knee will come up to the inside of your body at a 45° angle.

Extend the leg.

Use your hips to pull the leg across the front.

As you reach just inside the opposite 45° angle, retract the leg.

Set down. ◆

Axe Kick

The Axe Kick is not only a strong technique, but it is also used as a transition into a kick or trick combo. The most common is the Switch Axe Kick, which propels you forward into the next move.

 Important Notes

Be sure to pivot on your base leg for greater extention.

Your toes should be pointed as you bring your leg down.

Don't slam your foot into the ground after the kick.

Axe Kick

▶ Start in a Side
Fighting Stance.

Slide your lead foot back
as you step in front with
your back foot.

Raise the leg on a 45° angle
and bring it to the front.

Swing the leg down as
you point your toes on
your kicking leg and
pivot your hips.

(i) When you do this
kick correctly, the
toes of your kicking
leg, and the heel of your
base leg should be pointing
to the same direction.

Set down. ◆

67

Skip Front Kick

The staple of all routines. Even today a Skip Front Kick is common in extreme forms. Why? Because it is a great transition move from the ground into the air. It is a momentum builder.

Prep

Start: Right Forward Stance

1. Bring your Left knee up just like you are going to throw a Front Kick.

2. Push off your Right leg and bring up your Right knee, as you set the Left leg down.

3. Set the Right leg down into the same Right Forward Stance you started with.

All of the same notes from the Front Kick apply to this kick plus one more: After you retract your knee be sure to keep your knee up after the retraction, and step forward with that foot. I see a lot of people who Skip Front and swing the whole leg back with their leg still retracted and then step out. It takes too long, and it will kill any momentum.

Other things to keep in mind

When you switch your knees in step 2, you will actually skip into it (hence the name). **Do not** set one leg down then bring the other up.

The higher you drive your first knee up, the more lift you will have, and the higher you will skip. However, you will move slower.

For tricking you want to keep the skip low and fast.

Skip Front Kick

▶ Start in a Forward Stance.

Bring your back knee up just like you are going to throw a Front Kick.

Push off your base leg and bring up your opposite knee, as you set the other leg down.

Kick and retract with the leg you just brought up.

Set the kicking leg down into the same Forward Stance you started with. ◆

02 Standing Kicks

Taking your Kicks to the next level
General Guidelines

► **Height**

Kicking to the waist level might look good, but if you wish to show off *flexibility* and *strength* try kicking higher. To do so, pick your knee up higher before kicking.

To build up height, I suggest doing conditioning exercises (page 152).

Don't sacrifice technique for height. Remember that a great kick to the chest that has all the correct steps, looks better than a kick to the head with bad technique.

► Locking

Locking a kick is like freezing a frame. It shows the highest level of **strength** and **control**. Squeeze the quads (top muscles on your leg) to stop the kick, and finish by pulling it back.

This one is tricky because it takes a lot of leg strength to:

1. Get the leg up.
2. Extend the kick completely.
3. Hold it.
4. Retract the kick as fast as you threw it.

 You lock a kick at the moment of impact, at full extension.

► Posture

Every performance sport focuses on posture. Posture is not only technically important, but it is also directly related to your mood and how other people regard you.

If you walk around slouched over, you will begin to feel like how you look: unmotivated. No one will want to watch you, because no one wants to feel unmotivated or down. If stand up tall and walk proud, you will feel empowered and strong. People will be captivated by you and react to you differently.

 Be sure to always keep good posture when you are training. Your technique will be better and your overall performance and workout will be better as well.

Work both sides! Don't even think about only kicking with your best leg. You have to work both!

Tricks

JUMP FRONT KICK

JUMP SPLIT SNAP KICK

KICK THRU ROUND HOUSE KICK

SPIN HOOK KICK

TORNADO BENT KICK

TORNADO STRAIGHT KICK

TORNADO ROUND KICK

360 CRESCENT

HAND STAND

CAPOEIRA KICK

SWITCH CAPOEIRA KICK

CAPOEIRA KICK VARIATIONS

WAGON CARTWHEEL

2-HAND CARTWHEEL

1-HAND CARTWHEEL

DIVE CARTWHEEL

AERIAL

KIP

Jump Front Kick

The Jump Front Kick always seems to make its way into a form either to end a combo, cover the ring to set up for another combo, or to end a routine. This kick is fairly easy to do and it is rather explosive. What I see new today is the Jump Front Kick being used to switch from linear combos to spinning combos, and vice versa.

(i) It is a good idea to work on locking on the ground first, as it is the same idea in the air. As you kick, you will squeeze your leg muscles and freeze the kick in the air. Depending on how much air time you have, you might land on your non kicking leg before you retract the kick. This is fine. Just make sure to retract the leg to complete the kick.

Jump Front Kick Prep

▶ Step forward with your best leg. Arms in front.

Step your opposite foot forward and bend your knees as you draw your arms back.

Jump up extending your arms up.

As you reach the peak of your jump, pull your arms in and bring up your best kicking leg into a Front Kick position. At the same time, tuck your opposite leg in.
Land on your non-kicking leg, and finish with your kicking leg forward. ◆

Jump Front Kick

▶ Ready Stance.

Step forward with your
best leg. Arms in front.

Step your opposite leg
forward and bend your
knees as you draw
your arms back.

Jump up extending
your arms up.

As you reach the peak of
your jump, pull your arms
in and bring up your best
kicking leg into a Front Kick
position.

Kick and retract as you
tuck your opposite leg.
Land on your non kicking
leg, and finish with your
kicking leg forward. ◆

Jump Split Snap Kick

There are **many variations** of the Jump Split Kick. Each has its own special purpose. In this volume we will practice one variation.

Even though it is just one step up from a Jump Front Kick, a good Split Kick will also help with tricks such as Crowd Awakeners and the X-Out.

Jump Split Snap Kick Prep

▶ Step forward with your best leg. Arms in front.

Step your opposite leg forward and bend your knees as you draw your arms back.

Jump up extending your arms up.

Bring both knees up to your sides like a Horse Stance. Land on both feet at the same time. ◆

Jump Split Snap Kick

▶ From a Ready Stance step forward with your best leg. Arms in front.

Step your opposite leg forward and bend your knees as you draw your arms back.

Next, jump up extending your arms up.

As you reach the peak of your jump, pull your arms down and bring both knees up. It should look like a horse stance.

Snap two Front Kicks to either side.

Land on both feet at the same time. ◆

81

Kick thru Round House Kick

This kick will teach you the mechanics of how to generate power in all of your spinning kicks. This in turn will help you develop tricks faster. We will work on generating power by using your whole body and turning your hips over. The goal is to develop **power** and **momentum** by moving your whole body in a circular motion to kick. This technique is very similar to how Muai Thai kickboxers throw their powerful leg kicks.

Important Notes

Work the move one step at a time before putting it all together. This move takes time to really perfect. There is a lot to coordinate to generate the most power.

As I kick, I pop off the ground a little bit with my base foot. The lift helps me pivot easier.

Try to imagine yourself as a coil. When you start, you are a loose, uncoiled wire. Then as you kick, you twist up like a wire being coiled, and as you finish, you will explode out of the coil and return to your start position.

How do you know if you are turning your hip over? Look in the mirror. When you kick, if your base legs heel, butt, chest, and head are facing the mirror, and your hips and torso are to the back, you are correct.

Kick thru Round House Kick

▶ From a Side Fighting Stance turn your hips to the front, and prep your arms in the opposite direction of the kicking leg.

Bring the knee up and kick (Just like you would a regular Round Kick).

As you kick, turn your hips over by pivoting on the base foot so the heel aims to the front.

At the same time your arms should pull in the opposite direction of the kick.

Try to keep the leg the same level all the way to the back and then bring it down **with no retraction**.

Use your arms, which should still be to the front, to whip your upper body around bringing you back to the stance in which you started. ◆

Spin Hook Kick

This move is the mirror image of the Kick Through Round Kick. We are going to try to develop more power and greater extention with our Hook Kicks by using the whole body.

Important Notes

Try to keep the leg the **same level** throughout the kick until you are about to put it down.

You should feel the kick whip (or build momentum) two times:
One as you pull the kick across the front.
Two as you pull the kick to the back.

Use your upper body
To help you move through the kick faster, it is important to use your upper body too. As you begin the kick your **arms will be extended** to the outside. As you execute the spin, **your arms come in** and close to your body. As you finish the kick **your arms will stay in** to help you back to your start position.

Spin Hook Kick

▶ From a Side Fighting Stance, turn your hips to the front and prep your arms to the opposite side of the kicking leg.

Pull the arms across your body as you begin to spin.

Bring your knee up and start a regular Hook Kick, but instead of retracting, pull the leg across the front and all the way to the back.

Use your arms to whip
your body back into your
start position. ◆

Tornado Kicks

With Spinning Jump Kicks, things will get a bit more difficult. Now you have to jump, spin, kick, and land! The most common difficulty is taking off.

The Tornado Kick is the next progression after the Round Kick or the Kick Through Round Kick. It is an important kick to master before learning the 540. Again there are a lot of different ways to execute this kick, and each of them will help you achieve different results for tricking and forms. The first version of the Tornado Kick is with a Bent Leg Crescent Kick. After you learn the mechanics, we will explain all the fun and exciting variations.

We will work on 3 variations of the Tornado Kick. Everyone looks good doing different techniques. See what variation works best for you!

Tornado Bent (Leg Crescent) Kick
Tornado Straight (Leg Crescent) Kick
Tornado (Lock) Round Kick

Prep

Start: Side Fighting Stance

1. Turn your hips to the front as you prepare your arms to the Right side.

2. Use that prep to help you turn the opposite direction. As you continue to turn on your Right leg, jump and bring your Left leg up.

3. Continue the move by bringing up the Right leg in a Crescent Kick position.

4. You will land on your Left leg. Set the Right leg (which will be your kicking leg) behind you, opposite of your start position.

Arms:
Keep your arms spread out to start, and then bring them in tighter for speed as you are in mid jump.

Height:
To get the max height on this kick, it is important to drive your Left leg up.

For simplicity sake we will work step by step on one side, but it is important to make sure you work both sides

Tornado Bent Kick

Pros and Cons: This kick is faster then the other tornado kicks, and is easier to trick out of, but it does not show really good extension.

▶ Start in Right Side Fighting Stance. Turn your hips to the front as you prepare your arms to the Right side.

Pivot in a circle as you jump and drive your Left knee up.

Continue the move by
bringing up the Right
leg in a Crescent kick
position.

Snap the Crescent Kick and
retract as you land on your
Left leg.

You will land on your
Left leg. Set the Right
leg behind you. You will
now be in a Left Side
Fighting Stance. ◆

Tornado Straight Kick

Pros and Cons: This kick will show good extension, but it is slow.

▶ Start in Right Side Fighting Stance. Turn your hips to the front as you prepare your arms to the Right side.

Pivot in a circle as you jump and drive your Left knee up.

Do not chamber your Right
leg. Simply execute a
Straight Leg Crescent Kick.

You will land on your Left leg. Set the
Right leg behind you. You will now be
in a Left Side Fighting Stance. ◆

Tornado Round Kick

(i) **Pros and Cons:**
This kick is a great way to end combos and will show off great extension, but it is harder to generate any momentum to move into another trick.

▶ Start in Right Side Fighting Stance. Turn your hips to the front as you prepare your arms to the Right side.

Pivot in a circle as you jump and drive your Left knee up.

Bring your Right leg up horizontally for a Round Kick.

Continue the move
by extending the
Round Kick.

You will land on your Left leg.
Set the Right leg behind you.
You will now be in a Left Side
Fighting Stance. ◆

360 Crescent

The 360, or Jump Outside Crescent Kick, uses a two foot take off to generate height and power. The first prep we will work on is from a standing position. This will make sure we are doing the technique correctly before we practice stepping into it.

Standing Prep for the Jump Outside (360) Crescent Kick

Start: Left Side Fighting Stance

1. Turn your hips to the front as you prepare your arms to the Left side.

2. Use that prep to help you turn the opposite direction. Bend your knees and push off both feet at the same time. Bring both knees up and pull your arms in to help you spin.

Note: You can also start with straight legs and then work on tucking both legs.

3. You will land on both of your feet at the same time, in the stance you started.

Arms:
In step two, as you bend your knees, bring your arms in at a 45 degree angle, and lift them up at a 45 degree and angle as you jump.

Stepping Prep for the Jump Outside Crescent Kick

Stepping into the move will help you develop height, power and speed.

Start: Left Side Fighting Stance

1. Step forward with your Left leg into a Left Horse Stance as you prepare your arms to the Left side.

2. Bend your knees and push off both feet at the same time. Bring both knees up, pulling your arms in to help you spin.

Note: You can also start with straight legs and then work on tucking both legs.

3. You will land on both of your feet at the same time in a Left Side Fighting Stance.

Arms:
In step two, as you bend your knees bring your arms to the side at a 45 degree angle and then lift them up at a 45 degree and angle as you jump.

360 Crescent

▶ Start in a Left Side Fighting Stance. Turn your hips to the front as you prepare your arms to the Left side.

Bend your knees and push off both feet at the same time.

Bring both knees up.

Extend the Outside
Crescent Kick and retract.

You will land on both of your feet at the
same time, in the stance you started.
If you land on your Left leg first, that is
OK. You will be able to land correctly
if you work on your height. ◆

Variations

There are tons of different things you can do with this kick after you have the movement down. Here are a few:

>> Jump Outside Crescent Kick Gyro

Movement: In this move you will try to add a whole extra rotation to the Jump Outside Crescent Kick before you land.

Why it is cool: It will help you begin to prep for a Hurricane Kick (Double 720 Kick).

 Tip: After kicking, straighten your body out, and then try to turn. It is easier to spin when your body is straight.

>> Jump Outside Crescent Kick, one foot landing

Movement: This is the same as the Jump Outside Crescent Kick, but on your landing, land on your kicking leg.

Why it is cool: This is a great prep into another move. For example, a swing through Gainer (very advanced).

 Tip: Pull the kicking leg down to the floor straight. As you kick pull the opposite leg back to be ready for the next move.

>> Jump Outside Split Crescent Kick

Movement: The kick is the same as the Jump Outside Crescent Kick, but in step 2 instead of tucking your knees up, you will swing your legs in a split kick position.

Why this is cool: Just look at it, it is cool!

 Tips: People get stuck on this move because they do not start the jump spin prior to bringing the legs up.

Hand Stand

This move is all about balancing on your hands.

As you begin to Hand Stand, remember your body is strongest in one straight line. Any breaks on that line will be where you crumble.

When getting started, try practicing a Hand Stand against a wall. The wall will provide support and help you find your balance.

⚠ Use a spot when you begin to go all the way to a Hand Stand.

If you are going to tip forward, bend your arms, tuck your chin, and roll out of the Hand Stand so you do not land on your back.

Hand Stand Prep

▶ Start with your body straight and arms locked as straight as possible above your head.

Step forward and begin to reach for the ground, bending at the waist. As you bend at the waist, raise your back leg. It should be in line with the rest of your body.

As you place your hands on the ground, kick the base leg off the ground and bring your back leg up as straight as you can. Practice this exercise until you gain strength and confidence to hold both feet up.

As you come down bring one leg down first then the other, keeping your body straight. ◆

Hand Stand

▶ Start with your body straight and arms locked as straight as possible above your head.

Step forward and begin to reach for the ground, bending at the waist. As you bend at the waist, raise your back leg. It should be in line with the rest of your body.

As you place your hands on the ground, kick the base leg off the ground and hold both feet together at the top.

⚠️ Keep your head positioned so it follows the line of your spine. If you look too far forward, your feet will come down to the back. If you look too far back, you will fall forward.

As you come down bring one leg down first then the other, keeping your body straight.

Return to start position. ◆

Capoeira Kicks

Craig
Henningsen,
Sideswipe
Performance
Team member.

I love the Capoeira Kick. It really adds a whole other dimension to tricking. Once you have a strong Hand Stand, move on to Capoeira Kicks.

Capoeira Kick

Prep From Hand Stand

1. Start by facing the direction you want your kick to go. Begin your Hand Stand.

2. After you are up side down, lift the hand of the leg with which you want to kick. For example if you kick with the Right leg, then lift the Right hand.

3. Rotate your hips, and let the Right leg drop into the kick

4. Come down by placing the opposite foot on the floor and standing up.

INCORRECT

CORRECT

Correct Hip Aligment

The rotation of the legs from the hip sockets is very important for proper execution of the Capoeira Kick.

INCORRECT: Your knee and flexed foot are rotated in and facing to the side.

CORRECT: Your knee and foot rotated out.

Exercise Tip:
Without tilting your hips, raise your leg straight up. Rotate in, then rotate out. Repeat this motion until your muscles "memorize" the feeling.

Capoeira Kick Partner Drill

▶ **Spotter:** Hold the hand your partner will not be placing on the floor.
Kicker: Keep the arm you will place on the ground locked above your head.

Spotter: Help Control your partner into a Hand Stand.
Kicker: Keep your body in line as you reach for the ground.

Spotter: Continue to help control your partner as they do the Capoeira Kick.
Kicker: Swing your legs into a Hand Stand and let the kicking leg drop.

Spotter: Guide your partner back to start position.
Kicker: Return to start position with your body straight. The non-kicking leg will come down first. ◆

(i) If you are having trouble getting your capoeira kick to swing over, be sure that you let your hip turn over and not let it swing from the side. It should come over like a Front Kick position and not a Side Kick position.

Capoeira Kick (Au batido)

▶ Place opposite arm of kicking leg in the air.

Reach for the floor swinging the opposite leg over your body.

Important: Work up to having the leg go completely over your body. Start by having the leg come up half way, and then let it swing over more as you gain strength and confidence.

Return to standing. ◆

Switch Hand Capoeira Prep

▶ Start with your kicking leg forward, and the arm of your opposite side up.

Step your kicking leg back as you swing your arms in a circular motion. You will be in the reverse of your start position.

As you continue the circular motion with your arms, bend at the waist and reach forward with the forward arm. As you do this you will simultaneously lift your front leg starting your Hand Stand.

Continue to circle the arm that is not on the ground until it reaches the ground, as you swing the other leg up and go into a Hand Stand.

As you come down bring one leg down first then the other, keeping your body straight. Return to standing. ◆

Switch Capoeira Kick

▶ Start with your kicking leg forward and the arm of your opposite side up.

Step your kicking leg back as you swing your arms in a circular motion. You will be in the opposite position of your start position.

As you continue the circular motion with your arms, bend at the waist and reach forward with the forward arm. As you do this you will simultaneously lift your front leg starting your Hand Stand.

Continue to circle the arm that is not on the ground until it reaches the ground. Switch hands as you open your body to the front and drop the kicking leg.

As you come down the non-kicking leg will land first as you return to standing. ◆

Capoeira Kick Variations

Straight Leg   **1 Leg Tucked**   **2 Legs Tucked**

Shooting both Legs Up **Holding non-kicking Leg** **Split** **Flexed Foot**

Cartwheels

Before progressing to an Aerial, it is important to work on a good Cartwheel. An Aerial would be hard to do without a good Cartwheel, which is hard without a good Hand Stand. Cartwheels are fairly simple and safe to work on, and you will get a lot of mileage out of the technique.

Wagon Cartwheel
It may look a little silly, but this prep will help you get the feeling of the movement. In the Wagon Cartwheel pretend there is a big metal X in your body so you will be straight the whole time.

2-Hand Cartwheel
The reason you learn Cartwheels this way is so you can step forward into the move and not have to turn sideways to do the Wagon Cartwheel.

1-Hand Cartwheel
After practicing the 2-Hand Cartwheel, it is time to take it one step closer to an Aerial by removing one hand.

Dive cartwheel
This version of the cartwheel will help you develop your timing for your Aerial and add in the proper arm movements for maximum synergy in your body.

Wagon Cartwheel

Start hands and feet spread apart (you should look like a big X).

Push off and lift your Right leg placing the Left hand on the ground. Place the Right hand on the ground and bring your Left leg up.

Bring the Right leg down and the Left hand up. Place the Left leg on the ground, and bring both hands up returning to the start position.

ⓘ I know it sounds like the game 'Twister', but look at the pictures. If you don't feel comfortable with your legs going straight over the top, you can let them go to the side until you feel more confident.

2-Hand Cartwheel

▶ Step forward (we will start with the Left leg) and bring both arms up.

Bend at the waist and reach for the floor with both arms as you begin to bring up your Right leg.

Your Left arm will touch first and then your Right as you continue the motion with your Right leg.

Your Left leg follows your Right. Be sure to stay straight on one line.

Place the Right leg down and then the Left as you lift your chest and bring both arms up.

The finish position will be facing the opposite direction you started. ◆

1-Hand Cartwheel

▶ Step forward (we will start with the Left leg) and bring your Left arm up.

Bend at the waist and reach for the floor with your Left arm as you begin to bring up your Right leg.

Continue the motion with your Right leg as your Left leg follows the Right leg.

Be sure to only touch your Left hand on the perpendicular line of the direction you were going.

Place the Right leg down and then the Left as you lift your chest.

You should be facing the opposite direction. ◆

Dive Cartwheel

▶ Step forward (we will start with the Left leg) and bring both arms up in the air (like you are going to go into a Hand Stand).

Bend your Left leg as you begin to bring your arms around in a circle.
(picture from the front view)

As you push off the Left leg, your Right leg should be lifting. Your arms will continue to pass through the circle, turning your hips around to the opposite direction.

Both hands will land at the same time, on the perpendicular line of the direction you where going.

Place the Right leg down and the Left will follow, and you should be facing the opposite direction as you bring your chest up. ◆

Aerial

There are three different ways to throw this move. Here are some pros and cons of each one.

Spinning

You will step in a circle and Aerial.

Pro: Spinning into an Aerial makes it easier to build momentum. Plus it feels less scary to practice. This movement will be used in 90% of the combinations you will do.

Con: Normally what will happen with newer trickers is that the legs will not come straight over the top, but off to the side. The movement will look more like a Butterfly Kick than an Aerial.

This version of the Aerial will look good from the front, but will not look good from a side angle.

Elbows in

Step into the Aerial like you would step into a Wagon Wheel Cartwheel, and at the last second pull up your hands so only your elbows are out.

Pro: For this version of the Aerial you are building forward momentum with your upper body as you reach for the ground with your straight arms.
Con: All of your energy will be directed towards the ground so you will need to rely on your legs to do all of the work.

The Scoop

This version of the Aerial is the best way to learn, and the most accurate. You will be able to do all of the other variations of the Aerial if you can do this version.

Pro: This Aerial will help you keep your legs straight.
You will use more of your hamstrings and quadriceps muscles, as opposed to your abductors and adductors (like you would in the elbows in version).
You will be in the best position to trick out of (Aerial Twists)
Con: This is a seemingly harder move because it is all about getting the timing correct on your moves.

Aerial (The Scoop)

▶ Step forward (we start with the Left leg) and bring both arms up in the air.

Bend your Left leg as you begin to bring your arms around in a circle.

As you push off the Left leg, your Right leg should be lifting. Your arms will continue to pass through the circle, turning your hips around to the opposite direction.

The momentum should carry you through the move as you drive your legs over, and pull your arms in to help lift you.

Place the Right leg down and the Left leg will follow. You should end facing the opposite direction. ◆

Cartwheel and Aerial Drills

▶ Tapping

After you start feeling comfortable with the One Handed Cartwheel, you can work on tapping the floor. Begin the move like you are going to do a One Handed Cartwheel, but instead of placing your hand directly on the floor, try to begin the Aerial. After you start the Aerial, place your hand on the ground. Each time you feel confident putting your hand down try to place the hand down later and later, until you are able to get all the way over without touching.

▶ Whipping

Getting your legs to fly over your head is something your body was not meant to understand. To help your body understand this new movement, we will practice whipping. Whipping is moving your legs through your cartwheel as fast as you can.

Be sure you have enough room! Start by doing a Cartwheel. The second you start, try to whip your legs down to the floor as fast as you can and bring your hands over just as fast. You should be able (by the second or third cartwheel) to really feel the whipping motion of your body. It will feel like you don't need your hands.

I like to mix this one up and try Cartwheel, One Handed Cartwheel, and then Aerial. See what works best for you.

▶ Lifting

A lot of people will forget to use their legs when they are working on this move. Try the Dive Cartwheel with no step. Really focus on bending and pushing off your lead leg. Try placing a small mat or kicking shield under your foot and then pushing off. You will notice how much more lift you will get if your leg is bent.

Sometimes getting your body to understand how the trick feels is 90% of the battle.

 Warning! Be sure to be careful not to crush your partner's wrists or pull their shoulders.

Aerial Partner Drill

▶ **Spotter:** Position yourself facing the same side as the kickers front foot, and hold the kicker's hand that is crossing the body.
Kicker: Start from your strongest side in a forward stance. Cross hand over body and hold spotter. Bring the opposite hand up in the air.

Spotter: Guide and support the kicker through the entire motion of the Aerial.
Kicker: Bend the base leg and extend as you swing your back leg through the range of motion of the Aerial. Pull your arm to help you lift.

Spotter: As kicker completes the move be sure they don't over rotate.
Kicker: Finish with both hands up. ◆

Kip

The Kip is a move that will help you get off the ground faster and more dynamically then just standing up. This is actually one of the first tricks I learned. It is a cool move and one you can work without a partner.

The Bridge

What does a Bridge have to do with a Kip? The bridge is actually the center part of a Kip. Working on a good Bridge will develop back flexibility and strength.

1. Start on your back.

2. Place your legs shoulder width apart and your knees bent.

3. Your hands will be next to your ears (fingertips towards your body).

4. Extend your arms and your legs to create an arch with your torso. Be sure your arms and legs are fully extended.

Enrichment
Try to stand up from this position. It is hard, but this is the exact movement of the Kip, only slower. Also try going from a standing position and arch yourself back into a Bridge.
A partner is recommended for support for your back.

Kip Prep

▶ This move is all about timing and momentum. Start on your back with hands next to your ears and fingertips facing towards your body.

Keeping your legs straight swing them back until you are on your shoulder blades. Then simultaneously swing your legs forward and extend your arms.

Land in a Bridge position with your back arched. Stay arched. If you don't keep your back arched and bring your chest forward, your butt will go right to the floor. ◆

Kip

▶ Start on your back with hands next to your ears and fingertips facing towards your body.

Swing your legs back until you are on your shoulder blades.

Simultaneously swing your legs forward and extend your arms.

As your feet land, keep your back arched until your center of gravity is over your feet.

Bring your arms and chest forward to balance. Next stand up. ◆

Variation: If you have a flexible back, you can stay arched until you stand up.

Why walk
when you can fly.

Workouts

01 Workouts

Repetition is the key. Be sure to really take your time in perfecting these moves. Remember, it is not 'practice makes perfect', it is 'perfect practice makes perfect performance'. You don't want to just skim over these moves and practice them poorly, because you will create bad habits. Be sure to focus on performing all of your moves with proper technique.

I always get a lot of questions about how to train properly to do tricks. So here is the workout I do every day I train. This routine will help you continue to develop better technique and prepare your body to do more advanced moves.

Matt teaching class Sunday morning at Tarzana Karate, CA, 2006.

>> Basic Kicks Workout

All of these kicks you can do in place or stepping. Performing your moves in place is good if you don't have a lot of space, and stepping will help you create more fluidity while moving from one step to the next. Work both legs.

	Front	Round	Side	Hook	Inside Crescent	Outside Crescent	Axe
REPS	10	10	10	10	10	10	10
SETS	1	1	1	1	1	1	1

>> Spinning Kicks Workout

All of the spinning techniques we do in one place will be done in this part of the workout..

	Kick Thru Round	Tornado Kick	Spinning Hook
REPS	10	10	10
SETS	1	1	1

>> Spinning Kicks Combo Workout

Each kick in the combo should aim to different directions. The first kick will be at the Right 45 degrees angle, the aecond directly to the front, and the third to the Left 45 degrees angle.

	Spin Hook, Round, Spin Hook	Spin Hook, Round, Tornado	Spin Hook, Tornado, Spin Hook
REPS	3	3	4
SETS	1	1	1

Spin Hook

Round

Spin Hook

Spin Hook

Round

Spin Hook

02 Timing

What is timing?

In every trick, and every move, there is a perfect timing harmony that your body has to coordinate in order to perform the move. For example, let's take an Aerial. Your body needs to be able to:

1. **Swing one leg up**
2. **Bend and push off your other leg**
3. **Bring your arms around**
4. **Lift**
5. **Move each leg through the air**
6. **Land**

All of this has to happen in 1 second. This is the timing for the move.

How do I get better timing?

The way to improve timing is to breakdown each part and work on it separately. When you notice one part is not working, go back and work on that individual part of the move again.

Jackson Spidell, Sideswipe performer, 2006.

03 Plyometrics

Knee tuck jumps during Matt's class at Tarzana Karate, CA, 2006.

>> The Hops

With every step you take, your body makes millions of calculations to make sure you don't fall over. So get used to jumping before you go off, catapulting yourself in the air, and trying to kick and land.

>> Take Offs

Two Feet Take Offs

Two feet take offs are used primarily for height and power such as a Split Kicks and Jump Front Kicks.

One Foot Take Offs

One foot take offs are mostly used for spinning kicks such as Tornado Kicks

Spinning Take Offs

Spinning take offs are primarily done off two feet such as Jump Crescent Kicks.

Vertical Jump

10 jumps

1 Step forward with your best foot. Arms in front.

2 Step your other foot forward and bend your knees as you draw your arms back.

3 Jump up extending your arms up. Land on both feet at the same time.

>> Jumping Kicks Workout

Add a Skip Front Kick to these jump kicks to help you practice combinations and make a smooth transition from the ground to jumping.

	Skip Front, Jump Front prep	Skip Front, Jump Front	Skip Front, Jump Split prep	Skip Front, Jump Split	Skip Front, Jump Split, Jump Front
REPS	10	10	10	10	10
SETS	1	1	1	1	1

>> Jump Spin Kicks Workout

The Jump 360 should be worked stepping forward and when you do the kick you should add the Shuffle Axe to work transitions from the ground into the Jump Kicks.

	Jump 360 Prep	Axe, Jump 360
REPS	10	10
SETS	1	1

>> Acrobatics Workout

Caution should be emphasized when performing any acrobatic technique. Take your time and be sure you have proper matting. If you still have not gotten all of the moves, it does not mean skip it. Do the prep or one of the more simple variations. When practicing the Hand Stand, hold each one as long as you can then come down controlled. When practicing the Cartwheel Whip, try to develop whipping power in your legs by touching the hands first then feet to the floor as fast as you can all the way down the floor space.

	Hand Stand	Cartwheel Whip	One hand Cartwheel	Aerials	Capoeira Kicks	Kips
REPS	10	10	10	10	10	10
SETS	1	1	1	1	1	1

04 Conditioning

To achieve faster results in your training it is important to condition your body.

>> Push-ups

Push-ups are great full body exercises. You are using every part of your body to balance while working your arms, chest, and upper back. You can take a break between each set of 25.

	Regular Push-ups	Knuckles	Diamond	Wide	
REPS	25	25	25	25	
SETS	1	1	1	1	

Regular Push-up
Focus on deepening the chest

Knuckles Push-ups
Helps strengthen the wrists. Use the first 2 knuckles only.

Diamond Push-ups
focus on the Triceps.

Wide Push-ups focus on widening the chest.

>> Sit-ups

Every move you do in one way or another works your abs, so it is important that they are strong. In all of these exercises be sure to keep your neck neutral. You don't want to pull and strain your neck.

	Crunches	Crunch pull knees in	Single Crunch w/ knee pull in	Bicycles	Hollow Body
REPS	25	25	25	50	hold 1 min
SETS	1	1	1	1	1

Crunches -Start lying on your back with your knees bent. Raise head and shoulders 4-6 inches off the ground. Return to start position

Crunch with pulling knees in - Start with knees up, squeeze your lower abs and pull your knees in as you sit up.

Single crunch with knee pull in - Start with one foot on the ground and the other in the air. Pull your knee in and touch it with the opposite elbow.

Bicycles - Start with both legs in the air and touch opposite elbow to opposite knees. As you pull one leg in extend the other leg out.

Hollow body - Start lying flat on your back. Next, raise your feet and shoulders 4-6 inches off the ground.

>> Jumping

These jumping drills work on plyometric principles. Be sure to keep your heels off the ground and your hands in (to focus on just your legs) and do all Four exercises without stopping. Rest and repeat Three times.

	Calf Raises	Hops (short jump)	Extensions (high jump, no tuck)	Tucks (high jump)
REPS	50	50	50	50
SETS	3	3	3	3

>> Split Kick Drill

To perform this drill, stand in one place and do a Split Kick. As you land, pop back up and repeat. Do 3 sets of 10 kicks.

In the Combo Drill, stand in one place and do a Split Kick. As you land pop back up and perform a Front Kick. You will land with your kicking foot forward. Rotate and repeat starting with the Split kick. If your Right leg is forward, you will turn Left. If your Left leg is forward, you will turn Right. Repeat until you have gone in a circle.

	Split Kick Drill	Split Kick and Jump Front Combo Drill
REPS	10	10
SETS	3	3

>> Kick Conditioning

These drills will help you strengthen your legs, improve your balance, and help with locking and height. All of these drills should be performed close to a wall, but you don't want to lean on the wall because you are also working on balance. You can touch the wall only to regain your balance if you are losing it.

Slow Kicks
For every kick, take Three seconds to extend, Three seconds to hold, and Three seconds to retract.

Fast Kicks
This is like plyometrics for your kicks. Do these kicks as fast as you can without stopping.

	Slow Front	Slow Round	Slow Side	Slow Hook	Fast Round	
REPS	10	10	10	10	50	
SETS	1	1	1	1	3	

>> Hand Stand

Hand Stand Wall Hold
To help strengthen your arms and work on balance, ease yourself against the wall, and hold for One minute. Rest and repeat Three times.

Hand Stand Up Downs
To control going into and coming out of your hand stand, practice going into your hand stand, and once you reach your peek, immediately come back down. Repeat Ten times without stopping, rest and repeat.

	Hand Stand Wall Hold	Hand Stand Up Downs	
REPS	hold 1 min	10	
SETS	3	3	

05 Cool Down

After you finish your entire workout it is very important to stretch. This is when you will gain the most amount of flexibility and work lactic acid out of your muscles to prevent soreness. Each stretch should be held for 8-10 seconds. Be sure to breathe and relax.

Splits (Center and Sides)

Hips and Groin Stretch

Lower Back Stretch

Abs Stretch

Shoulders Stretch

Calves Stretch

Hamstrings Stretch

Quads Stretch

Training is a journey
not a destination.
One of the greatest pieces
of advice I can give you is to
find the joy in the journey.
The journey is what makes
you who you are when you
arrive at your destination.
Enjoy the ride.

Workout Routines at a glance

>> Warm-up and Stretch

	Jumping Jacks	Jogging 1	Jogging 2			
REPS	100	30 sec	30 sec			

	Waist Rotations	Shoulders	Neck Stretches	Knees 1 and 2	Ankle	Wrist
REPS	10	10	10	10 each	10	10

	Lunges	Squats 1, 2, 3 and 4	Leg Swing 1 and 2	Hip Swing	Hamstring	Hip Flexor Stretch	Shoulders
REPS	10	10 each	10 each	10	10	10 sec	10 sec

>> Kicks and Jump Kicks

	Front	Round	Side	Hook	Inside Crescent	Outside Crescent
REPS	10	10	10	10	10	10

	Kick Thru Round	Tornado Kick	Spinning Hook	Hook Round Hook	Hook Round Tornado	Hook Tornado Hook
REPS	10	10	10	3	3	4

	Extension Jump	Skip Front, Jump Front prep	Skip Front, Jump Front	Skip Front, Jump Split prep	Skip Front, Jump Split	Skip Front, Jump Split, Jump Front
REPS	10	10	10	10	10	10

	Jump 360 Prep	Shuffle Axe, Jump 360
REPS	10	10

>> Acrobatics

	Hand Stand	Cartwheel Whip	One hand Cartwheel	Aerials	Capoeira Kicks	Kips
REPS	10	10	10	10	10	10

>> Conditioning

	Regular Push-ups	Knuckles	Diamond	Wide
REPS	25	25	25	25

	Crunches	Crunch pull knees in	Single Crunch w/ knee pull in	Bicycles	Hollow Body
REPS	25	25	25	50	hold 1 min

	Calf Raises	Hops (short jump)	Extensions (high jump, no tuck)	Tucks (high jump)
REPS	50	50	50	50
SETS	3	3	3	3

	Slow Front	Slow Round	Slow Side	Slow Hook	Fast Round
REPS	10	10	10	10	50
SETS	1	1	1	1	3

	Split Kick Drill	Split Kick and Jump Front Combo Drill
REPS	10	10
SETS	3	3

	Hand Stand Wall Hold	Hand Stand Up Downs
REPS	hold 1 min	10
SETS	3	3

>> Cool Down

Splits (Center and Sides)	Hips and Groin	Lower Back	Abs	Shoulders	Calfs	Hamstrings	Quads

Hold each stretch 8-10 seconds. Breath and relax.

TRICKS check list

- ☐ **Jump Front Kick**
- ☐ **Jump Split Snap Kick**
- ☐ **Kick thru Round House Kick**
- ☐ **Spin Hook Kick**
- ☐ **Tornado Bent Kick**
- ☐ **Tornado Straight Kick**
- ☐ **Tornado Round Kick**
- ☐ **360 Crescent**
- ☐ **Hand Stand**
- ☐ **Capoeira Kick**
- ☐ **Switch Capoeira Kick**
- ☐ **Capoeira Kick Variations**
- ☐ **Wagon Cartwheel**
- ☐ **2-Hand Cartwheel**
- ☐ **1-Hand Cartwheel**
- ☐ **Dive Cartwheel**
- ☐ **Aerial**
- ☐ **Kip**

> Avoiding Sports Injury

Training is fun and it develops fitness and coordination. But like with any sport, injuries can happen. However, about 50% of all sports injuries may be preventable if you take precautions before and during training.

Michelle Mix and Craig Henningsen, 2006.

Pre-Training Precautions

1. Talk with your doctor before starting any new activity. A physical exam can show potential problems or weaknesses that may affect your performance.

2. Practice conditioning exercises to build strength and flexibility as needed.

3. Warm up and stretch before practice to prevent injuries. Cool down after practice to avoid soreness.

4. Work up to exercises gradually. See the workout routine from this book as an example.

5. If you exercise outdoors during midday sun make sure to apply sunscreen every hour and drink plenty of water.

6. Avoid training when dehydrated, tired, or in pain, which can all increase the risk of injury.

It may not always be possible to prevent injuries, but taking extra precautions before and during practice can sure reduce your risk.

No Golfing
LAMC. 6344 (B.7)

TRICKING
se permite | in this
aqui | area

Index

TRICKS / 73

WORKOUTS / 143

Tricks
CITY LIMIT
POP 2006   ELEV 360

MAIL ORDER FORM

High Mountain Publishing
Tarzana Karate, 19618 Ventura Blvd, Tarzana, CA 91356
Tel: 818.705.KICK(5425)
Email: info@greatwarriorpak.com
www.HowtoTrick.com

CUSTOMER INFORMATION

Name (Ship to) _____

Address _____

City, State and Zip _____

Buyer (if different from above name) _____

Home or Cell Phone _____

Email _____
(we must have phone no. or email to confirm order)

CREDIT CARD ☐ M/C ☐ Visa ☐ AMX ☐ Disc

Card Number _____

Exp. Date _____ CVC(Security) Code _____

Signature as it appears on card _____

High Mountain Publishing
Learn | Master | Teach

Please make checks payable to:
Tarzana Karate
Credit Card Orders Call 818.705.5425
Mon-Sun 9:30am-9pm PST

Money Order and Cashier' s Check are accepted. Orders paid by personal checks will be delayed 2-3 weeks for clearing.

PRODUCT INFORMATION

Product Name	Qty.	Price
_____		$ _____
_____		$ _____
_____		$ _____

Shipping and Handling Info
International Orders Accepted;
US Currency only. $35.00
Shipping.
$25.00 Shipping for Canada
Customers.
For 2nd Day Air Shipping, add
$20 (Small packages only).
Wholesale orders - Email
info@greatwarriorpak.com for
shipping cost.

Subtotal _____

Sales Tax (Ca;8.25/7.75%)

Shipping $8 (1-5 books)

Add'l Shipping _____

TOTAL _____

Return Policy
Books and Merchandise will be accepted for return only if it is in "brand-new" condition. Return within 30 days of receipt. Wholesale returns within 14 days of receipt. No exceptions. All returns need to include a copy of original invoice for proper credit or exchanges. For complete terms conditions, and return policy visit our online stores at **tarzanakarate.com or howtotrick.com.**

High Mountain Publishing

Learn | Master | Teach